Questions You Never Thought You'd Ask

DID THE ROMANS EAT CRISPS?

And Other Questions About History

Paul Mason

Raintree is an imprint of Capstone Global Library Limited, a company incorporated in England and Wales having its registered office at 7 Pilgrim Street, London, EC4V 6LB – Registered company number: 6695582

www.raintreepublishers.co.uk
myorders@raintreepublishers.co.uk

Text © Capstone Global Library Limited 2014
First published in hardback in 2014
Paperback edition first published in 2015
The moral rights of the proprietor have been asserted.

Edited by Dan Nunn, Rebecca Rissman,
    and John-Paul Wilkins
Designed by Steve Mead
Original illustrations © Capstone Global Library Ltd 2013
Illustration by HL Studios
Picture research by Mica Brancic
Production by Sophia Argyris
Originated by Capstone Global Library Ltd
Printed and bound in China by CTPS

ISBN 978 1 406 25947 6 (hardback)
17 16 15 14 13
10 9 8 7 6 5 4 3 2 1

ISBN 978 1 406 25953 7 (paperback)
18 17 16 15 14
10 9 8 7 6 5 4 3 2 1

British Library Cataloguing in Publication Data
Mason, Paul.
Did the Romans eat crisps? and other questions about history. -- (Questions you never thought you'd ask)
902-dc23
A full catalogue record for this book is available from the British Library.

Acknowledgements
We would like to thank the following for permission to reproduce photographs: Alamy pp. 9 (© Ancient Art & Architecture Collection Ltd), 15 (© Lesley Pardoe), 23 (© akg-images), 25 (© imagebroker/Rosseforp), 27 (© North Wind Picture Archives); Corbis p. 7 (© Werner Forman); Getty Images pp. 16 (Keystone/Hulton Archive), 19 (The Bridgeman Art Library); Imperial War Museum p. 17 Monopoly set; iStockphoto pp. 14 Queen Elizabeth (© Steven Wynn), 14 toilet (© Rouzes); Library of Congress p. 13 (Prints and Photographs Division Washington, D.C. 20540 USA); Shutterstock pp. 4 potatoes (© Nattika), 4 Roman legionary soldier (© Nejron Photo), 4 brown bag (© Lim ChewHow), 5 pouring honey (© 12_Tribes), 5 dormouse (© Eric Isselée), 5 toast (© travellight), 6 Aztec man (© Vladimir Korostyshevskiy), 6 suitcase (© Stephen Coburn), 6 holiday photos (© maigi), 8 white statue (© Denis Kornilov), 8 sports shirt (© Polryaz), 8 sports shorts (© karam Miri), 10 hairdresser tools (© Rido), 10 Egyptian woman (© Sergei Butorin), 11 (© Rachelle Burnside), 12 skyscrapers (© gary718), ferry (© Hannu Liivaar), 17 metal files (© optimarc), German money (© Patricia Hofmeester), 17 old map (© Steven Wright), 17 compass (© Irina Tischenko), 18 (© Darren J. Bradley), 20 terracotta warriors (© bluefox), 21 football pitch (© Peter Baxter), 21 terracotta warriors (© Txanbelin), 21 football (© Quang Ho), 21 golden goal (© diez artwork), 22 French flag (© c.), 22 Belgian flag (© ArtisticPhoto), 22 chips (© Africa Studio), 24 old paper scroll (© Irina Tischenko), 24 egg (© Picsfive), 26 construction worker (© Elena Elisseeva), 26 garden wheelbarrow with gold (© Wire_man), 26 street paved with gold (© SueC), 28 Viking soldier (© Microprisma), 28 wooden house (© bioraven), 28 sports car (© Michael Shake), 28 fire stripe (© Jag_cz).

Cover photographs of a Roman legionary soldier (© Nejron Photo), a brown bag (© Lim ChewHow), and some crisps (© Africa Studio) reproduced with permission of Shutterstock.

We would like to thank Diana Bentley and Marla Conn for their invaluable help in the preparation of this book.

Every effort has been made to contact copyright holders of any material reproduced in this book. Any omissions will be rectified in subsequent printings if notice is given to the publisher.

CONTENTS

Did the ancient Romans eat crisps? 4

Did the Aztecs send postcards? 6

What kind of team kit did athletes wear
    at the original Olympics? 8

Should you shampoo a pharaoh? 10

Which city was built from ships? 12

Who was the first queen to use a toilet?.............14

How did prisoners of war pass the time? 16

Which horse had a city named after him? 18

Did ancient Chinese warriors play football? 20

Where did chips come from?................................22

Did people in ancient China wear nail varnish?.......24

Have a city's streets ever been paved with gold? ...26

Did the Vikings use satnav? 28

Glossary...30

Find out more 31

Index...32

Some words are shown in bold, **like this**. You can find out what they mean by looking in the glossary.

DID THE ANCIENT ROMANS EAT CRISPS?

That would be impossible! Crisps are made from potatoes, which originally came from South America. The first potatoes only reached Europe in the 1500s – hundreds of years after the Romans had left.

EMPIRE CRISPS

SMELLY SANDALS FLAVOUR

Did you know?

The Romans did like some very unusual snacks – including dormice! The mice were coated in honey and sprinkled with poppy seeds.

DID THE AZTECS SEND POSTCARDS?

No, they didn't! Firstly, **Aztecs** didn't really go on holidays. But more importantly, the Aztecs couldn't really write. Instead, they used pictures to communicate with each other. For example, 'night' would be shown with a black sky and a closed eye.

Did you know?

Aztec pictures do not run in order, like words in a sentence. They make up a giant picture puzzle, where lots of things can happen at once!

WHAT KIND OF TEAM KIT DID ATHLETES WEAR AT THE ORIGINAL OLYMPICS?

Athletes at the ancient Olympics had no team kit – because they didn't wear any clothes at all! Women athletes were **banned**. To make sure this rule was never broken, the athletes had to compete naked.

Did you know?

Women were allowed to watch the Games - as long as they were **supervised** by a man.

This ancient Greek vase shows Olympic runners competing without any clothes.

SHOULD YOU SHAMPOO A PHARAOH?

Pharaohs didn't need shampoo! Ancient Egyptians – especially important ones – usually shaved their heads. Then they put on fancy wigs. The bigger and more fancy your wig, the more important you were.

Did you know?
A golden razor found in Tutankhamun's **tomb** was still sharp enough to shave with despite being over 3,000 years old!

WHICH CITY WAS BUILT FROM SHIPS?

In 1848, gold was discovered near San Francisco, USA. People came from all over the world, hoping to become rich. Ships were abandoned in the harbour while the sailors ran off to look for gold! Local people used the ships to make all sorts of buildings.

Did you know?
Restaurants, shops – even the local jail was built from an old ship!

WHO WAS THE FIRST QUEEN TO USE A TOILET?

The first queen with a modern toilet was Elizabeth I. Her **godson**, Sir John Harington, built it. Harington's invention didn't catch on. After Elizabeth's death, the royal toilet was torn down.

One would leave it a while...

Did you know?

In the olden days, most toilets were wooden benches, with big holes in them. The waste dropped through the hole – usually into a river. Yuck!

HOW DID PRISONERS OF WAR PASS THE TIME?

During World War II, some British **prisoners of war** were sent board games by the people back home. But these were board games with a difference! Hidden inside were secret escape tools that they could use to escape from the German **POW camps** where they were being held!

I'm bored.

Game of Monopoly?

Items hidden in the Monopoly sets included metal files, money, a compass, and a map.

WHICH HORSE HAD A CITY NAMED AFTER HIM?

The horse was called Bucephalus. His owner was the Greek warrior-king Alexander the Great. Alexander spent his life conquering a huge kingdom. Bucephalus died in a battle far from home, in Pakistan. Alexander promptly named a new city after his beloved horse.

Welcome to
Horseville

Did you know?
Alexander the Great was just 13 years old when he **tamed** Bucephalus.

DID ANCIENT CHINESE WARRIORS PLAY FOOTBALL?

Yes, they did. One of the earliest forms of football was an ancient Chinese military exercise. It was called *Tsu Chu*.

To score, players kicked a ball into a net. The warriors would have been good at taking **penalties** – the net opening was only 30 to 40 centimetres wide!

Nice big goal ...

Yes, this looks simple!

WHERE DID CHIPS COME FROM?

Chips probably came from France – though some people claim it was actually Belgium. The first chips didn't look like they do today. When rivers and lakes froze, people could not catch fish to eat. Instead they cut potatoes into fish shapes and fried those.

Did you know?
American soldiers developed a taste for 'French fries' during the First World War.

DID PEOPLE IN ANCIENT CHINA WEAR NAIL VARNISH?

Yes, they did. The first nail colouring was probably used in China about 5,000 years ago.

Recipe for ancient Chinese nail colour:
1. Mix beeswax, gum, colouring, and egg white
2. Paint on nails

Hey presto – you've had an ancient Chinese makeover!

Did you know?
In ancient China, long fingernails showed you were important – too important to do physical work!

HAVE A CITY'S STREETS EVER BEEN PAVED WITH GOLD?

In the 1500s, stories told of an African city so rich that the streets were paved with gold. Its name was Timbuktu. Timbuktu's streets were never actually paved with gold – but it was very rich. Timbuktu was a centre for the trade in salt and... gold.

Did you know?
The first **Westerner** to see the city of Timbuktu arrived in the 1820s.

DID THE VIKINGS USE SATNAV?

Vikings loved to travel. But they didn't use satellites. In fact, satellites weren't invented for another 1,000 years.

But the Vikings did have a few navigation tricks:
1. Direction finders used the Sun's position to decide a course.
2. Sunboards used the Sun's shadow to work out **latitude**.
3. Sunstones located the Sun when it couldn't be seen.

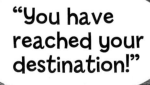

"You have reached your destination!"

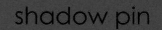

shadow pin

shadow

course
indicator

By lining up the Sun's shadow with the course indicator, the Vikings coud use sunboards to stay on the right course. But they were not much good when it was cloudy!

GLOSSARY

Aztecs group of peope who lived in central Mexico hundreds of years ago

banned not allowed; against the rules

godson male person who an older person has promised to help and guide through life

latitude measure of how far north or south you are

penalties in football, a penalty is a kick at goal taken from 12 yards (11 metres) away. Penalty kicks are defended only by the goalkeeper.

POW camp place where prisoners of war are held during a war

prisoner of war person captured by the enemy during war

supervised watched over to make sure things were done in the correct way

tamed no longer wild; made friendly to humans

tomb place where a dead body or bodies are kept

Westerner someone who lives in the West, particularly Europe or North America